Contents

School grounds can provide the stimulus for a wide range of mathematical investigations and activities. This book contains photocopiable worksheets for pupils to use which fulfil National Curriculum requirements for mathematics at Key Stage 2. Many of the worksheets are suitable for pair or small group work as well as individual work. Some of them are best tackled, in part at least, as a whole class activity with different pupils contributing different parts.

The worksheets are divided into five sections reflecting the main areas of mathematics taught at Key Stage 2: Number Counting, Number Pattern, Measurement, Shape and Space, and Data, with ideas for trails at the end. They have been written with a variety of schools in mind – those with well developed school grounds, those with basic school grounds provision, those in rural and urban areas. Brief teacher's notes are provided below highlighting any issues of safety, suggesting extension ideas and indicating any particular skills which need to be taught before a sheet is tackled.

This pack follows on from the very successful book for teachers, *Mathematics in the School Grounds* by Zoe Rhydderch-Evans, and credit must go to her for many of the ideas. If you would like to develop your school grounds further, contact the Learning Through Landscapes Trust, 3rd Floor, Southside Offices, The Law Courts, Winchester, Hampshire SO23 9DL.

Teacher's Notes

A symbol ⚠ on a worksheet is designed to alert pupils and teacher to a potential danger. Please see the notes below and explain to your pupils how to take care.

NUMBER COUNTING
1. Looking at the Building
- If your school does not have visible bricks, you could use panels, or count roof tiles (from a distance!) instead. Or use another nearby brick building.
- You need to find out or guess the cost of one brick first.
- Extension – children can devise their own worksheets on number counting for each other.

2. Choosing What to Count
- Encourage pupils to choose different things to count so that you can discuss their findings together as a class afterwards.

3. Counting Words
- Extension – pupils look for other mathematical words in a dictionary and make a class collection of such words, or perhaps even a mathematical picture dictionary, with a picture as well as, or instead of, each definition.

4. Pathways and Visitors
- This sheet involves the drawing of a plan to scale. It also uses average and percentage.

NUMBER PATTERN
5. How many Bricks in a Wall?
- If your school is not made of bricks which are visible, find a brick wall elsewhere.

6. Shooting Goals
- Extension – pupils could devise more complicated ways of scoring or of playing a goal-shooting game.

7. Leaves
- Best done in autumn when fresh leaves can be collected from the ground. Remember to warn the class not to damage plants.
- Uses area by counting squares, and averages.

8. Squares and Plants
- You will need enough string for each

group to make a square. You will also need additional string to demonstrate how much is needed for bigger sized squares. You will need an area of grass.

MEASUREMENT

9. Shadows Challenge

- This needs a sunny day, when shadows can be seen on the ground. The activity will disrupt the day, as measuring needs to be done at different times through the day, e.g. early, mid-day, mid-afternoon. It is best begun in the first session of the morning.
- Extension – measure the shadows of other things such as trees or buildings.

10. Birds' Food

- Provide or ask pupils to bring to school a variety of bird food. The best way to measure how much the birds eat is to measure the food before you put it out, and then either note when it has all gone, or measure it again later.
- Weighing amounts of different things, such as apple, seeds, bread, will be useful.
- To decide which birds eat most you could record the amount of time each is seen feeding, but larger birds will eat more in a given time.
- To measure how much the birds drink you could measure how much the container holds, and then note when it is empty or measure what is left later. But remember, if the weather is warm evaporation will occur, and if you leave it overnight you do not know what else has drunk from it.

11. Weather

- You could keep a three-month record by having a rota. Each pair in the class record for about one week.
- See *Science in the School Grounds*, published by Southgate Publishers, for ideas on how to make a raingauge, and instruments for measuring wind direction and strength. To measure sunshine think about the number of hours of sun

in the day and the amount of cloud cover.
- Extension – home-made measuring devices could be compared with real weather instruments and techniques, looking at accuracy and precision.

12. Our School Buildings

- This involves drawing a rough plan and then a plan to scale, also perimeter and area.
- Extension – to calculate the space per pupil more accurately, measure the thickness of the walls, take this away from the outer measurements and work out the inside floor area. You could also take away the space taken up by the inside walls.

SHAPE AND SPACE

13. Minibeast Shapes

- Remind pupils to treat minibeasts with care. They should preferably not be touched or moved, but drawn in situ. If they must be moved, then handle them very carefully and replace them carefully where they were found.
- This involves symmetry and right angles.
- Extension – comparing other man-made and natural shapes and patterns.

14. Angles

- Pupils will need a protractor, pen and paper for each pair.
- This involves measuring angles.
- Safety – you may want to warn pupils not to climb to measure angles.
- Extension – this could be developed into an angles trail.

15. Length and Breadth

- Remind pupils to take care when measuring doors in case someone is coming through. Best done at a quiet time of day.

16. Shape Detectives

- It is important that the first part of this is done individually, otherwise the partner can't enjoy working out the clues.

- Pupils need to know their basic shapes.

17. Pathways
- This involves drawing a plan.
- Extension – design a questionnaire to ask visitors or others about the paths and routes they use.

DATA
18. Habitats Survey
- Remind pupils to treat minibeasts with care. They should preferably not be touched or moved, but drawn in situ. If they must be moved, then handle them very carefully and replace them carefully where they were found.
- Discuss different types of habitats in the school grounds before tackling the worksheet.
- Extension – work on probability.

19. Plants Survey
- Have some plant catalogues or reference books available to help pupils think about any plants they might want to add, and in which to look up the likely heights of plants.

20. Running Challenge
- Safety – be aware of any pupils with asthma or similar problems.
- A stop watch would be useful.

21. What Goes in the Bin?
- Safety – pupils should NOT handle rubbish except with plastic or rubber gloves. It is very important to brief the pupils about the safety aspect of this.

- You will need plenty of plastic or rubber gloves and plastic bags, preferably all the same size.
- Uses percentages and pie charts.
- Extension – you could also conduct a daily class waste bin survey.

22. Water Challenge
- This is perhaps best done as a class activity, with different groups of pupils contributing different elements. Perhaps 6 groups.
- Safety – finding how much water is used in one flush requires close supervision, and is only possible if the school has toilets with low cisterns. It is probably a good idea to involve the caretaker to help you to do this activity.
- Emphasise the safety aspects of reducing the amount of water we use WITHOUT reducing hygiene.
- Extension – pupils could do the same for their own home.

TRAIL
23. Shapes
- Emphasise that the trail should follow a safe route.

24. Counting Eye-Spy
- Emphasise that the trail should follow a safe route.

25. Visitors' Trail
- Extension – combine the best ideas from the different trails to make one Visitors' Trail for the school, and invite visitors to use it.

1. Looking at the Building

Take a pen, paper and clipboard outside.
Walk round the school building.

1 Look at it carefully. Estimate first and then count. How many walls are there? How many windows?
How many bricks were used to build each wall? (Count one row. How many rows?)

2 How many bricks, to the nearest hundred, were used to build the school? (You might find it helpful to draw up a table with one column for each wall. Don't forget to allow for the windows!)

	Number of Bricks	
	Estimate	**Count**
Wall 1		
Wall 2		
Wall 3		
Wall 4		

3 If each brick costs £....... how much did the walls cost?

Draw a chart or table to record your results.

	Number of bricks	**Cost of each brick**	**Cost of bricks in the wall**
Wall 1		£..........	
Wall 2		£..........	
Wall 3		£..........	
Wall 4		£..........	

4 Look at the building and invent three counting questions for a partner.

2. Choosing What to Count

Get ready to go outside. Take a pen, paper and clipboard with you.

1 Choose something outside to count, of which you think there are more than five but fewer than fifty; for example, trees.

Write down what it is: ....

Write down the number you estimate there are:

....

Are you right? Count and write the number here:

....

2 Choose something of which you think there are more than 200 but less than 500.

Write down what it is: ....

....

Write down the number you estimate there are:

....

Are you right? Count and write the number here:

....

3ᵃ Fill in the table below. List things to count outside.

3ᵇ Which list is longest?

....

3ᶜ What do you notice about the physical size of the objects in the 'ones' column compared with those in the 'thousands' column?

| | Best counted in: | | |
ONES	TENS	HUNDREDS	THOUSANDS

3. Counting Words

The words in the box below are all 'counting words'. What do they mean?

COUNTLESS   A LOT

A FEW   **sundry**   none   **umpteen**

many

A HANDFUL   INNUMERABLE   several

SOME

myriad   **nil**   host   multitude

1 Guess the meaning first. Then use a dictionary to look up any you do not know.

2 Put a ring round those that mean a large number. Put a line under those that mean a small number.

Go outside and look around.

3 Choose two of the words you have ringed. Write a sentence for each word, about something you can see outside.

4 Choose two of the words you have underlined. Write a sentence for each word, about something you can see outside.

5 Choose three other words from the box. Draw a picture for each one to show the number of things they describe.

4. Pathways and Visitors

1 Draw a plan of the school's paths.

- Draw a rough plan first. Then measure the paths.
- Estimate the total length of paths or routes.
- How long is the path from the gate to the main entrance? Mark these measurements on the rough plan.
- Decide on a scale and draw your plan.
- Then use your plan to work out the total length of paths or routes.

Label the main routes A, B, C, etc. for example:

Route	
A	Gate to main entrance
B	Main entrance to Caretaker's shed
C	Car park to main entrance
D	

2 In groups, tally the number of people using each route in a day. Can you find a way to distinguish how children, adults who work in the school and visitors are recorded?

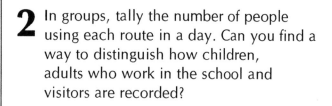

The above tally equals 17.

3 Which are the most popular paths? Can you show this in a table or graph?

4 What is the average number of visitors in a week? What percentage of these come in through the main gate?

5. How Many Bricks in a Wall?

1 Draw a table to show the number of bricks needed to build a wall up to 10 rows high, but with 8, 9, 10, 11, 12, bricks in each row.

Number of bricks in each row	Number of rows high									
	1	2	3	4	5	6	7	8	9	10
8	8	16	24	32						
9	9	18	27	36						
10	10	20	30	40						
11	11	22	33	44						
12	12	24	36	48						

2 Go outside and look at a brick wall. Estimate and then count the bricks in a row. Estimate and then count the rows of bricks from the ground to the top.

3 Draw a table to show the bricks needed to build a wall the size of your wall, and twice as long, 3 times as long, 4 times as long, 10 times as long.

4 Explain what happens when you increase the size of the wall.

6. Shooting Goals

1 In pairs go outside and take it in turns to practise shooting goals. Each person has five shots at a time. Keep a tally of your partner's shots and goals scored.

Round of shots:	Goals scored	Points per go	Total Points
1	1	5	5
2	5	30	35
3	2	10	45
4			
5			

If you score 1 award 5 points.
If you score 5 goals out of 5 shots you score 5 extra points.

What will you score for 8 goals in 8 shots?

Is this a fair way of scoring?

2 Make up another interesting way of scoring. Write it down here

....
....
....
....
....
....
....
....
....

3 Draw a table to show your partner's results using both scoring methods.

7. Leaves

Get ready to go outside. You will need a ruler, squared paper and a pen.

1 In your pair collect together 10 different leaves. Remember not to damage any plants. If possible collect leaves from the ground. Measure and record:
The axis of each leaf.
The width of each leaf.
The area of each leaf in squares.

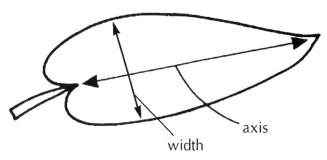
axis
width

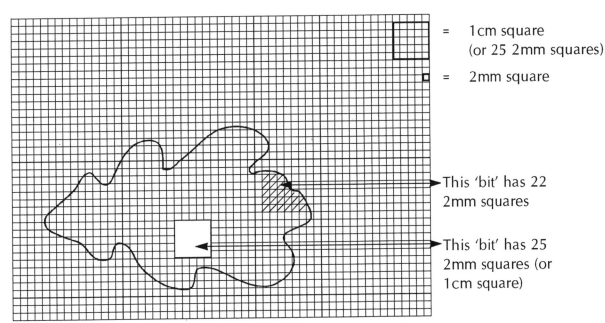

☐ = 1cm square
(or 25 2mm squares)

▫ = 2mm square

This 'bit' has 22 2mm squares

This 'bit' has 25 2mm squares (or 1cm square)

2 Make a table like this one:

	Type of leaf	Axis	Width	Area
1	Oak	3cm	1cm	.....
2				
3				
4				

Is there any pattern in the numbers in your table? Does it vary for different types of leaves?

3 Work out the average measurements of your leaves. What is the average size of all the leaves found by the class?

Ribwort

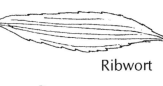
Dandelion

Creeping buttercup

Daisy

Hawkweed

8. Squares and Plants

1 We use four equal pieces of string to make a square. How many pieces do we need to make a square with sides twice as long? Three times as long?
Show this in a diagram. Go up to 8 times as long.
What pattern can you see in the number of pieces of string needed?

3 Choose the square size you think is best. Go outside and count the different plants in different places (where people walk, under trees, near a fence, in an open sunny place).
Make a table to compare the number of plants found in each place.

2 What size of square do you think will be best for counting plants in grass?
Go outside and count the different plants using different sizes of squares.

Make a table to show your findings.
Is there a relationship between the size of the square and the number of plants found?

Squares	Size	Number of plants found
1	30 x 30 cm	
2	60 x 60 cm	
3		
4		

Children counting plants inside a square.

9. Shadows Challenge

On a sunny day go outside in pairs.

1 Measure the length of your shadows.
What is the best measuring tool for this?
Do this at different times through the
day. What times would be best?

2 Choose another shadow to measure too.
Fill in this table:

Length of shadows			
Time	**My shadow**	**Partner's shadow**	**Other shadow**

3 You could also measure the shadow
widths and make a table.

4 The second time you go out, measure
the length of your own shadow. Then
see if you can estimate the length of the
other shadow you have chosen.

Do you notice any pattern in the lengths
of the shadows?
Do you notice any pattern between the
lengths and widths of the shadows?

10. Bird's Food

Feed the wild birds each day for a week. Try seeds, apple pieces, cheese, bread. Where is the best place to put their food? Why?

1 Record how much the birds eat. Try to decide which birds eat the most. How can we make a good estimate rather than just guessing?

2 How much water do the birds drink? Why is this difficult to measure?

3 Work out how much seed the birds would eat in a year. (Do you feed them all year round?) How much does bird seed cost? How much do we need to spend on bird seed each year?

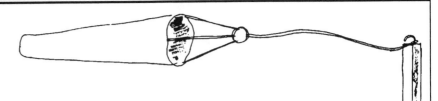

As a class keep a record of
weather measurements over
three months.

1 Design and make a weather calendar for
each month. Allow enough space against
each day to record your measurements.

FEBRUARY 1998						
Mon	**Tue**	**Wed**	**Thur**	**Fri**	**Sat**	**Sun**
						1
2	3	4	5	6	7	8
9	10	11	12	13	14	15
16	17	18	19	20	21	22
23	24	25	26	27	28	

2 How could you measure rainfall?
Keep records of your measurements.
Compare the rainfall from week to week.
What is the average rainfall per day?
What is the most rainfall in one day?
What is the least?
Draw a graph.

3 What materials would be best to measure
wind strength?
What weight of materials would be best?
Try materials of different weights.
Can you design a method of measuring
wind strength?

4 Design a way of measuring sunshine.
Design a table to record sunshine.

12. Our School Buildings

1 Go outside and, in groups, measure the perimeter of the school buildings. Measure the length of each outside wall, including any doors.

2 Draw a rough plan of the outside walls. Mark each wall on your plan with its measured length. Make sure you have drawn on and measured all the outside walls. Do you have all the measurements you need to draw a plan to scale?

3 Draw a plan to scale of the school buildings, using cm² paper. Choose a suitable scale, perhaps 1cm on the paper to 1 metre on the ground.

4 Use your plan to work out the area of the school. This is approximately the same as the floor space inside the school.

5 How many pupils are there at the school? How can you find out?

6 Calculate the amount of floor space per pupil. Divide the total area of the school by the number of pupils. Estimate and then measure and draw in chalk outside on the ground, the area for one pupil.

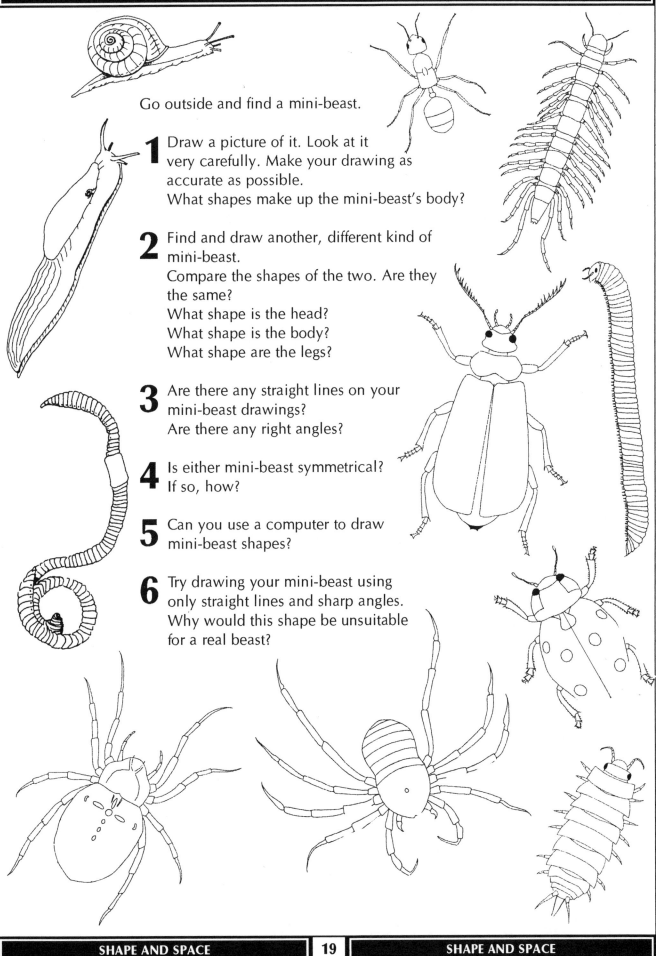

Go outside and find a mini-beast.

1 Draw a picture of it. Look at it very carefully. Make your drawing as accurate as possible.
What shapes make up the mini-beast's body?

2 Find and draw another, different kind of mini-beast.
Compare the shapes of the two. Are they the same?
What shape is the head?
What shape is the body?
What shape are the legs?

3 Are there any straight lines on your mini-beast drawings?
Are there any right angles?

4 Is either mini-beast symmetrical?
If so, how?

5 Can you use a computer to draw mini-beast shapes?

6 Try drawing your mini-beast using only straight lines and sharp angles.
Why would this shape be unsuitable for a real beast?

14. Angles

Get ready to go outside. You will need a protractor, pen and paper. In pairs look at angles.

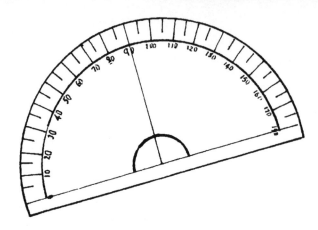

1 One person identifies an angle. Their partner estimates the size of the angle. The first person then measures the angle. After 5 angles, change over.

Make a table like the one below. An example is done for you.

Angle place	Estimate	Measurement
Herb bed corner	90°	85°

2 Work out a way of deciding which of you came closest in your estimations.

15. Length and Breadth

Go round the school building, inside and out. Find as many different doors as you can.

1 Estimate and then measure the height, width and thickness of each different door.
Is there any pattern in the numbers?
Are short doors always narrower?

2 Look for patterns in measurements (e.g. length and width) of other things. Try natural things, such as leaves, or plants. Make a chart to record your measurements. Then look for patterns in the numbers.

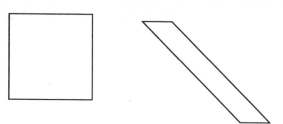

1 Go outside. Walk round your school building and grounds. Find the following shapes and write where they are. Do this ON YOUR OWN.
Make a chart like the one below to record this.

Shape	Where found
Rectangle	
Triangle	
Circle	
Oblong	
Square	
Cube	

If possible find two other shapes of your own. Write them in the space.

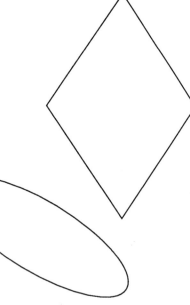

2 For each shape you have found write a clue so that a friend can find it. For example, for the rectangle: 4 sides, not all equal. We come and go through it. The answer would be a door.

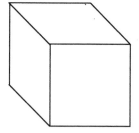

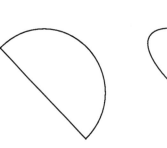

3 Can you put your shape clues together into a shape trail? The person following the trail should be able to go from one shape to the next, following your clues.

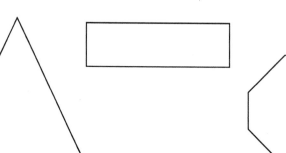

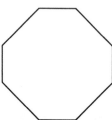

17. Pathways

1 Draw a plan of the school boundary. Mark the main gate and any other gates. Draw the buildings and the main doors.

2 Design a pathway system around the school. Will your paths be straight or curved? Why? What kind of corners will the paths have? Will people stick to your paths or will they take short-cuts across grass or flower beds?

3 Describe the shortest route round the school. Describe the longest route.

4 Take your plan outside. How are your paths different from the existing ones? Can you mark the real ones on your plan with dotted lines?

5 Go outside (a) in dry weather, (b) in wet weather, and watch how people use the paths. Now try to make some suggestions for improving the existing paths.

1 Find out which habitats different mini-beasts like.
Which ones like dark or light? Make two lists.
Which ones like wet or dry? Make two lists.

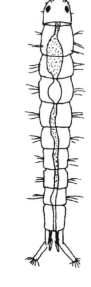

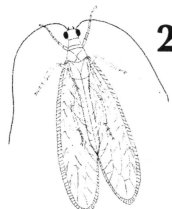

2 Make a survey
of different habitats
in the school grounds.
Decide what types of habitat
to survey.
Decide how to record where
different mini-beasts are found.

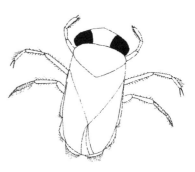

3 Choose one type of mini-beast. Compare
the numbers of your chosen mini-beast
in different habitats.
What is the average number
in each habitat?
What habitat area has
the most?
What habitat area has the least?

4 Can you estimate
the probability of
finding your chosen
mini-beast in the
following habitats?

Habitat	Likely to find	Unlikely to find
Dry and dark		
Wet and dark		
Dry and light		
Wet and light		

Carry out a survey of the plants in the school grounds.
Think about what you need to take outside with you.

1 Can you find a way of counting or estimating the number of plants? Don't forget to include trees, shrubs, wildflowers and other plants.
Decide whether to count/estimate just the number of DIFFERENT KINDS of plants or the total of ALL the plants.

Go outside and do your survey. How can you record the results? Try using a plan or graphs.

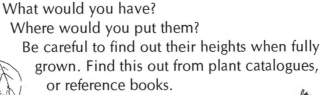

2 Now answer some questions about the plants in your school grounds.
How many trees are there over 1.5 metres high?
How many plants produce fruit?
How many plants are used for food?
How many plants grow to less than 4 cm in height?

3 Think about whether there are any plants you would like to add to the grounds.
Plan any trees or shrubs you would like to add.
What would you have?
Where would you put them?
Be careful to find out their heights when fully grown. Find this out from plant catalogues, or reference books.

20. Running Challenge

Set up a test to see how fast someone the same age as you can run round the field/playground.

1 Think about:
How many people do you need to test?
How are you going to do the test?
How are you going to make the test fair?
What things might affect how fast they run?

2 List the equipment you will need.
Make a plan for your testing.
Design a way of recording the test results. Do you want to record any other information apart from the name and time taken?

3 Make a chart from the results.

4 Can you predict whether you would get the same results:
(a) on another day,
(b) with a different class,
(c) with pupils the same age from a different school?

21. What Goes in the Bin?

Did you know that 30% of the contents of an average home dustbin is paper and card? What percentage of the school dustbin contents is paper and card? Can you estimate?

Before you go outside you should each have a plastic carrier bag and you should each protect yourself from germs by wearing rubber gloves.

1 How can you find out what percentage of the school dustbin is paper and card? What other materials are there? Make a list.

Decide how you are going to sort the materials. Decide on four or five categories (e.g. paper and card, plastic, glass, other waste).
How will you compare the amount of paper and card with other materials? (Weight? Number of pieces? Number of bags filled?)
Everyone needs to use the same method of sorting, and the same method of counting the amounts. Sort the materials into the categories you have chosen. Then count how much there is of each category of material, and the total amount of material.

2 Back in the classroom record your findings. Draw a pie chart to show the percentages of different categories of materials.

3 Will the rubbish contents be the same every day?
How can you find out the average or a typical day's contents?
Could any of the materials be recycled?

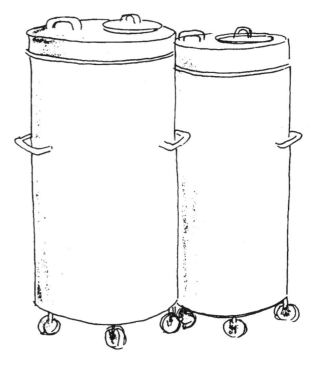

How much water does your school use in one day?

1 Toilets. How many times a day are they used? (Don't forget to include teachers!) You could work out an average for the number of times each person in the school uses the toilet in a day, based on asking your class, and then multiply this by the number of people in the school.
How much water is used for each flush? You could work this out by taking the lid off one cistern, flushing the toilet, holding the ball-cock up to prevent the water coming in, and then seeing how much water you need to pour in to the cistern to bring the water up to the normal level.

2 Washbasins. Can you find the amount used when you wash your hands?
How many times per day?
Is there a difference between using a running tap or water in the basin?

3 Estimate the amount of water used in classroom sinks, science lessons, etc.

4 Kitchens. Interview kitchen staff. How much is used for cooking and drinking water?

5 Cleaning the school. Interview the cleaners to find out how much they use.

6 Outside. How much is used for watering plants or other outside uses?

7 Other uses. Is there anything else?

Design a questionnaire to find out the answers to 4, 5 and 6 above.

8 Add up all the water used in one day. How much is used in one week? One year? Can you find out how much that costs the school?

9 Draw graphs to compare the different uses of water in school. What uses most water?

10 Are there any ways we could SAFELY cut down the amount of water we use?

23. Shapes

Make a trail for your friends using shapes in the school grounds. Start with easy shapes, such as squares, and go on to more difficult ones.

1 First go outside and find your shapes. Use directions to guide the trail users from one shape to another. For example: *From the classroom door walk straight ahead for five paces. Then turn and face left. What shape do you see?*

2 Ask the person following the trail to: draw shapes, or count shapes, or name shapes, or count their sides, or measure the longest side. Be as inventive as possible.

Remember to keep a record of the correct answers.

3 Try your trail out. It should take about 10 to 15 minutes to complete, carefully following the instructions.

4 Give it to a friend to try. How could it be improved?

24. Counting Eye-Spy

Can you make a trail in the school grounds based on counting?

1 Go outside. Draw a plan of the grounds. Mark each stop on the trail with an X and a number.
At each stop ask a counting question or give a number and ask what has been counted, for example:
You can see five here (Answer: windows)
How many trees can you count from here? (Answer: 4)

Ask them to add, minus, multiply or divide the things they can see.

2 To make it more difficult, you could ask the person doing the trail to multiply or divide one answer by another, for example:
What can you see here? Multiply the answer to question 2, by the answer to question 3. What can you see this number of?

3 Ask a friend to try out your trail. Are there any problems? Can you improve it?

4 Can you make an easy trail for the Reception or Class 1 children and a difficult trail for your class-mates or teacher?